Better Lives with Bionics

by Lee Wagner

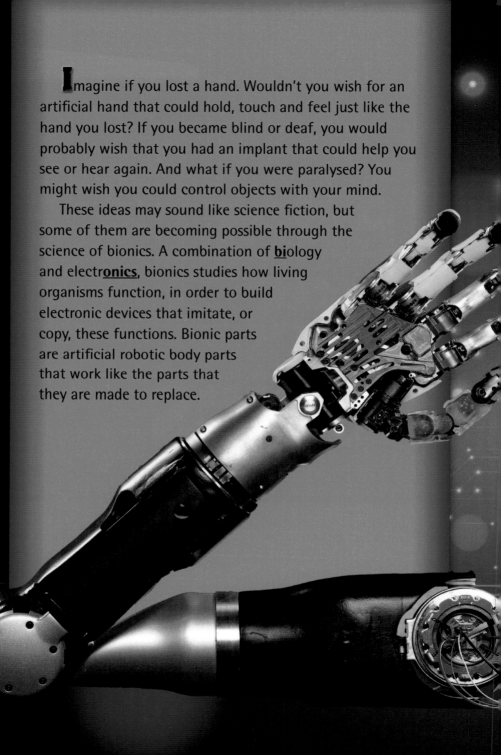

Imagine if you lost a hand. Wouldn't you wish for an artificial hand that could hold, touch and feel just like the hand you lost? If you became blind or deaf, you would probably wish that you had an implant that could help you see or hear again. And what if you were paralysed? You might wish you could control objects with your mind.

These ideas may sound like science fiction, but some of them are becoming possible through the science of bionics. A combination of **bi**ology and electr**onics**, bionics studies how living organisms function, in order to build electronic devices that imitate, or copy, these functions. Bionic parts are artificial robotic body parts that work like the parts that they are made to replace.

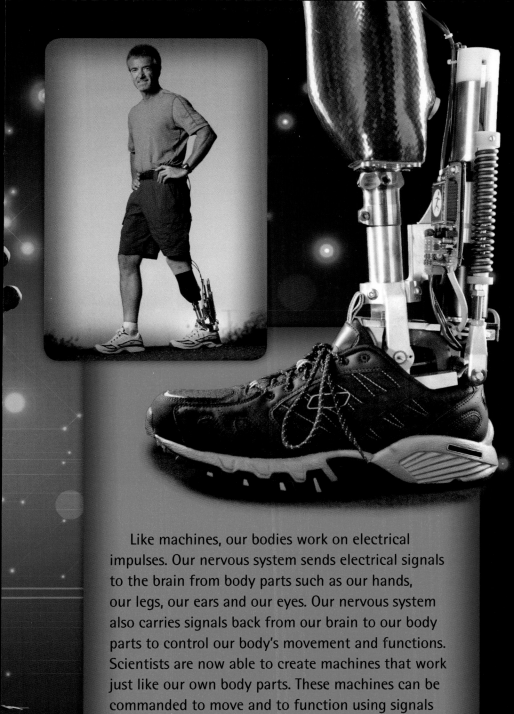

Like machines, our bodies work on electrical impulses. Our nervous system sends electrical signals to the brain from body parts such as our hands, our legs, our ears and our eyes. Our nervous system also carries signals back from our brain to our body parts to control our body's movement and functions. Scientists are now able to create machines that work just like our own body parts. These machines can be commanded to move and to function using signals from our brain!

This is Amanda Kitts. She lost her arm in a car accident in 2006. Although she has now only got a stump where her arm used to be, Amanda still remembers the whole arm and hand she used to have.

Scientists have connected electrodes and wires to the muscles in her stump. Then they attached an artificial, bionic arm to the stump. The electrodes pick up electrical impulses from the nerves in the muscle tissue in Amanda's stump. The impulses are sent from Amanda's brain when she thinks about moving the arm or hand she remembers. The bionic arm responds to her thoughts and moves in ways that are similar to a real arm!

The robotic arm is not easy to get used to. Amanda needs a lot of practice to be able to control her hand and make it perform the tasks she wants it to.

This technology is still very new and it isn't perfect. Scientists are working on the robotic arm to make it function better. They are developing sensors to help the user feel what he or she is touching or holding. In the future, this will make it easier for the user to have better control of movements. Eventually the user will be able to pick up small objects, such as a key, and squeeze objects, such as a bottle of mustard, without accidentally squeezing too hard!

Bionics are not only used to restore movement. They can also be used to help improve the function of other systems in our bodies, like hearing.

A bionic device called a cochlear implant can help a completely deaf person hear some sound again. The implant works by picking up sound with a microphone and changing the sound to electronic signals. Electrodes carry the signals from the microphone on the side of the head deep inside the ear to the cochlear nerve. This nerve is the part of the ear that controls hearing.

Unlike bionic arms and legs, the cochlear implant is not a very new technology. Over the past 30 years, nearly 200,000 people around the world have received cochlear implants.

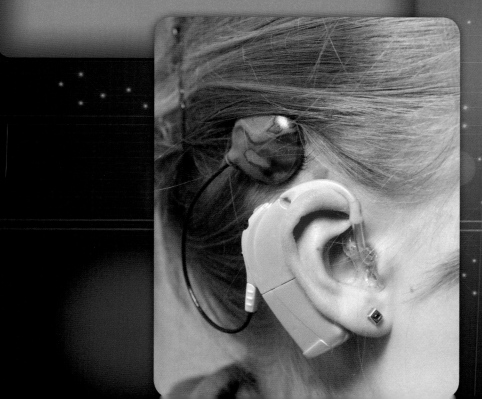

A little boy named Aiden Kenny is one of these people. Tammy Kenny, his mother, remembers finding out that her baby was deaf. She says, 'Once, my husband banged pots and pans together, hoping for a response.' Aiden did not hear the noise.

But he can hear anything now! When he was ten months old, doctors put cochlear implants in both of his ears. The day Aiden's implants were turned on, he started responding to sound. His mother remembers, 'He turned around at the sound of my voice. That was amazing.'

Hearing is not the only sense that can be improved through bionics. There is also a bionic eye implant that can restore some sight to blind people.

Like other bionic body parts, the bionic eye uses electrical impulses to send signals to the brain. Electrodes connected to the back of the eye send information to nerves in the brain. This information helps people like Jo Ann Lewis, who lost her sight years ago as a result of an eye disease, to see shapes and colours. The images are not very clear, but the implant does allow Jo Ann to recognise specific objects.

One of the last things Jo Ann remembers seeing naturally were trees. Today, she is able to see the shapes of trees again. Jo Ann says, 'Nowadays, I can see branches sticking out here and there.'

The bionic eye works a bit like a camera. The more electrodes that are connected, the better the image. Jo Ann Lewis' implants have got 60 electrodes.

Scientists are working on newer, better models that will have hundreds of electrodes. With more electrodes in place, people who receive the implant will be able to see even more clearly.

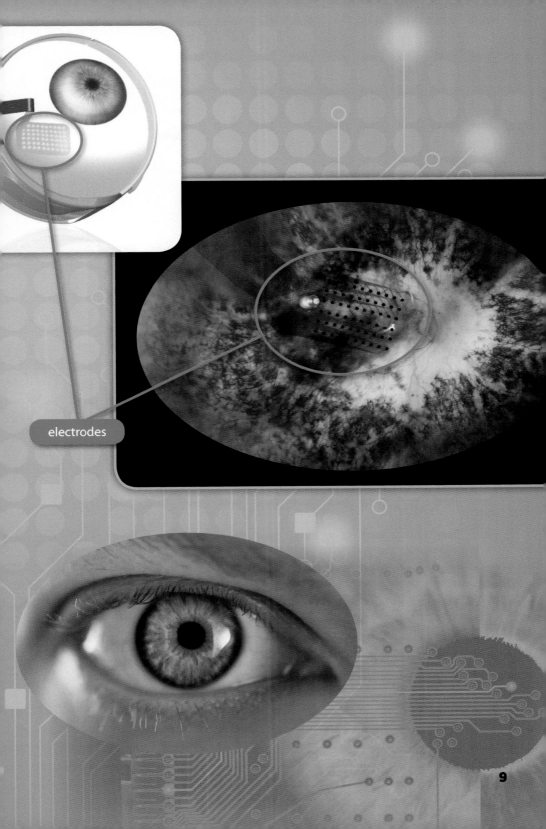

electrodes

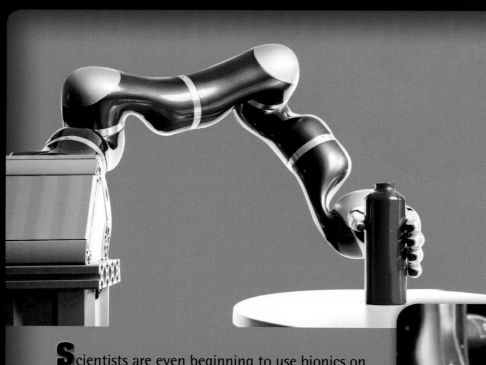

Scientists are even beginning to use bionics on the brain itself. The goal is to make it possible for paralysed people to control objects with their mind. So far, the people in the studies have been able to move a cursor around a computer screen and to control objects like televisions and robotic arms, like this one, with their mind.

The brain is extremely complex, and scientists have still got a lot to learn about it. But our knowledge of the brain is growing and technology is becoming more and more precise every day.

Each year, advances are made in bionic technology. Maybe many years from now bionic arms and legs will have been perfected. Maybe someday bionic ear and eye implants will restore full hearing and sight. And maybe paralysed people will even be able to move their own bodies using bionic devices.

Research in bionic technology has still got a long way to go. At the moment, bionic parts are only a rough imitation of the parts created by nature. But still, they give people who have lost the function of one part of their body a way of doing what their bodies used to be able to do naturally.

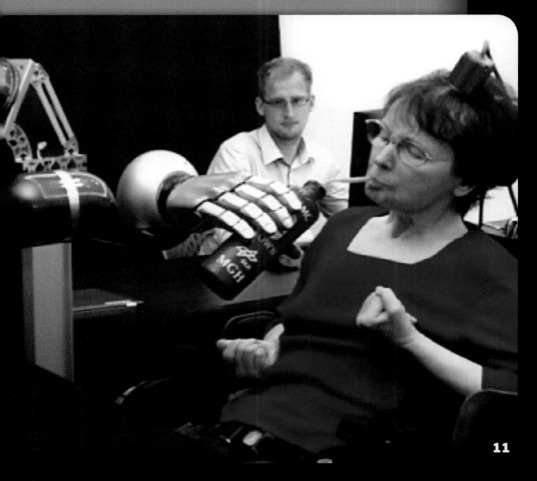

Facts About Technology and Disabilities

Most people can read emails, type messages on computers and speak to others. They don't think twice about being able to communicate in these ways. Yet people with disabilities may have trouble doing these things. Fortunately, there are technologies that can help.

People who are blind cannot see a screen. But they can still get email. How? Special programs have been created that change the text on a computer screen into speech so that a blind person can hear the information on a computer screen instead of having to see it.

In order to send a message, the person can use a speech recognition program. With this technology, as a person speaks into a microphone, his or her words appear on the computer screen. This technology is also extremely helpful for people who have disabilities that make it impossible for them to use their hands to type.

But what if a person hasn't got use of their hands or their voice? Technologies have been developed that allow people with severe disabilities to control a computer with only a slight movement of a part of the body like the head, a thumb, or even just by blinking or sniffing. A video camera above the person's monitor replaces a mouse and a keyboard. It picks up these slight movements, allowing the person to communicate through his or her computer!

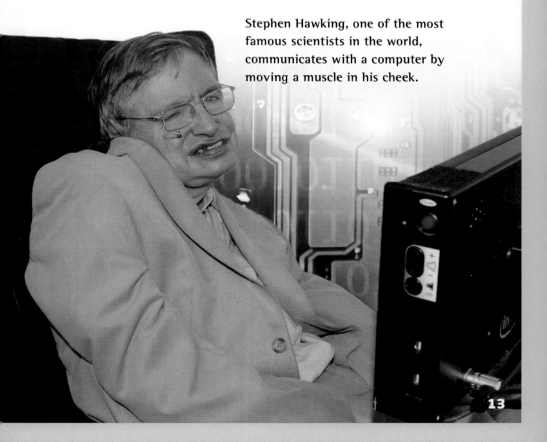

Stephen Hawking, one of the most famous scientists in the world, communicates with a computer by moving a muscle in his cheek.

Use the correct form of the words below to complete the paragraphs.

precise   control   task   complex
respond to   science fiction

Surgery of the Future

There is a new, amazing kind of surgery that may become common in the future. The surgery is done by a robot! With this kind of surgery, robotic arms can perform very difficult, __complex__ surgeries like heart surgery. This may sound like _____, but it is true!

Of course the robot does not do the surgery by itself. A surgeon sits at a computer that is often just a few feet away from the patient and carefully _____ the robotic arm as it operates on the patient. The robotic arm _____ the surgeon's movements, carrying out all of the surgeon's commands.

This surgery may be safer than surgery performed by a person. A robotic arm is able to be more _____ than human hands can be. A robot can complete the surgery by making smaller cuts than a human doctor can.

In the future, it is likely that more and more surgical _____ will be performed by these robotic arms.

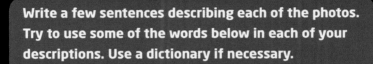

Write a few sentences describing each of the photos. Try to use some of the words below in each of your descriptions. Use a dictionary if necessary.

robotics   control   science fiction   precise
task   command   complex   respond to   program
voice recognition   sensor

Glossary

artificial made by man, not created naturally

biology the science and study of life

blind not able to see

cochlear nerve a nerve that carries signals related to hearing from the inner ear to the brain

devices things (usually electronic or mechanical) that are made to perform a particular task

disability a physical or mental condition that limits a person's movements, senses or activities

electrodes devices used to conduct electricity from one point to another

electronics the science of creating tiny electrical devices

function work

implant something that has been put inside a person's body

impulses small amounts of energy

nerves parts of a system in the body that control physical feeling and movement

nervous system the network of nerves that transmits nerve impulses between parts of the body

paralysed not able to move

signals actions or things that send a message, usually without words

stump the shortened part that remains after something is cut (from something such as a tree, an arm or a leg)